Immortality In The Flesh

Prentice Mulford

Kessinger Publishing's Rare Reprints

Thousands of Scarce and Hard-to-Find Books
on These and other Subjects!

- Americana
- Ancient Mysteries
- Animals
- Anthropology
- Architecture
- Arts
- Astrology
- Bibliographies
- Biographies & Memoirs
- Body, Mind & Spirit
- Business & Investing
- Children & Young Adult
- Collectibles
- Comparative Religions
- Crafts & Hobbies
- Earth Sciences
- Education
- Ephemera
- Fiction
- Folklore
- Geography
- Health & Diet
- History
- Hobbies & Leisure
- Humor
- Illustrated Books
- Language & Culture
- Law
- Life Sciences

- Literature
- Medicine & Pharmacy
- Metaphysical
- Music
- Mystery & Crime
- Mythology
- Natural History
- Outdoor & Nature
- Philosophy
- Poetry
- Political Science
- Science
- Psychiatry & Psychology
- Reference
- Religion & Spiritualism
- Rhetoric
- Sacred Books
- Science Fiction
- Science & Technology
- Self-Help
- Social Sciences
- Symbolism
- Theatre & Drama
- Theology
- Travel & Explorations
- War & Military
- Women
- Yoga
- *Plus Much More!*

We kindly invite you to view our catalog list at:
http://www.kessinger.net

Immortality in the Flesh

WE believe that immortality in the flesh is a possibility, or, in other words, that a physical body can be retained so long as the spirit desires its use, and that this body, instead of decreasing in strength and vigour as the years go on, will increase and its youth will be perpetual.

We believe that the reputed fables in the ancient mythologies, referring to the "immortals," or beings possessed of powers other and greater than "mortals," have a foundation in fact.

This possibility must come in accordance with the law that every demand or prayer of humanity must bring supply. There is now a more earnest demand than ever for longer and more perfect physical life, because now more minds see the greater possibilities of life. They appreciate more than ever the value of living in the physical. Such demand often takes this form of expression, "I have just learned how to live and it is nearly time for me to die."

The body will grow to these results through a gradual series of spiritual processes, operating on and ever changing, spiritualising and refining the material.

These processes do not retain the body a person may have now. They retain "a body" and an ever-changing and refining body.

146

Immortality in the Flesh

All disease (lack of physical ease) or sickness comes of a spiritual process, the aim of which is the reconstruction of the physical body, first, in the receiving of new elements, and, second, in the casting out of old ones.

Back of this physical reconstruction, however, there is going on the far more important reconstruction of the spirit out of which is built the body.

These processes are continually going on with the body, operating through the skin, the stomach and other organs, as well as in the periods of physical prostration or indisposition above referred to.

All sickness is an effort of the spirit, renewed by fresh influx of force, to cast off old and relatively dead matter. But as this intent has not been recognised by the race, the spiritual process or effort, with its accompanying pain and discomfort, has been held and feared as a signal or approach of death. So, with no knowledge of spiritual law, and judging everything by the material, the temporary and necessary weakness of body accompanying the process has been considered an unmitigated ill. Such belief has in the past only aided the spirit to pile on itself more and more of belief in the untruth that after a certain term of years no power or force in the universe could prevent the physical body from "aging," shrivelling, weakening and finally perishing.

The body is continually changing its elements in accordance with the condition of the mind. If in certain mental conditions, it is adding to itself elements of decay, weakness and physical death. If in another mental condition, it is adding to itself elements of strength, life and perpetual life. That which the spirit takes on, in either case, is

147

thought or belief. Thoughts and beliefs materialise themselves in flesh and blood. Belief in inevitable decay and death brings from the spirit to the body the elements of decay and death. Belief in the possibility of an ever-coming inflowing to the spirit of life brings life.

If new life is being thus added to you, there must also be an accompanying throwing off of the old or relatively dead matter of the body, just as when an influx of new life comes to the tree in the spring, it casts off the dead leaves which may have clung to it all winter.

Through similar inflowing of new life or force does the animal and bird yearly shed the old fur or feathers and take on the new, and correspondent changes take place throughout the whole organisation of bird, animal and man.

The spiritual law works in all forms and organisations of the cruder form of spirit which we call "matter." In the human being this influx of force is greater than in the lower forms of life. It does not flow equally to all human beings. Some receive more than others. But in the course of advancement men and women are to come who will receive so much of this influx as to be obliged to see these further possibilities of existence and also to realise them.

When new ideas or thoughts are received by our higher mind or self, they are warred against by our lower or material mind. The body is the battle-ground between these two forces and therefore suffers. As minds come to trust, even to a small extent, in the Supreme Power and entertain the idea that physical disease and physical death are not absolute necessities, the higher Power must prevail. Some old error will be cast out; some new idea will come to stay; the body will be better and stronger after each succeeding struggle, and these struggles will also gradually become less and less severe, until they cease altogether.

People have in the past lost their physical bodies, because, being in ignorance of the fact that sickness is a process of the spirit to throw off the old material thought and take on new, they have used their forces in the wrong way to retain such thought. They retain it by their belief. Your belief will make your sickness a benefit or an evil to you. If you can but entertain the belief that it is a spiritual process of getting rid of old worn-out elements, you assist greatly the mind in the performance of this process. If, however, you believe that sickness is entirely a physical condition, and that no benefit and only evil comes of it, you are using force only to load down the spirit with more and more error, of which your flesh and blood will be in quality an expression, until at last your spirit rejects the body which it has been trying to carry and drops its burthen. It rejects at last the whole body through the same laws by which it rejects a part of it when that part is spiritually dead.

If you receive with scorn the thought that your physical body, through fresher and fresher renewal of its substance, can be made perpetual, you close to yourself an entrance for life and open another to decay and death.

We do not argue that you "ought" to believe this. You may be so mentally constituted that you cannot now believe it. There are many things to be in the future which none of us have now the power to believe. But we can, if the thing deemed impossible be desirable, pray or demand a faith which shall give us a reason for believing, and such faith will come in response to demand.

Faith means power to believe in the true, or the capacity for the mind to receive true thoughts.

The faith of Columbus in the existence of a new continent was a power in him to entertain an idea greater than others of his time. People who, to use the common expression, "have faith in themselves," have also an actual power for carrying out their undertakings greater than those who have no faith in themselves. When you demand faith in possibilities for yourself that now seem new and strange, you demand also the power and ability to draw to you the capacity to see or feel reasons for truths new to you. If you demand persistently the truth, and only the truth, you will get it, and the whole truth means power to accomplish seeming impossibilities.

"Thy faith hath made thee whole," said the Christ of Judea to a man who was healed. To us this passage interprets itself as meaning that the person healed had an innate power of believing that he could be healed. This power which was of his own spirit (and not of Christ's), so acted on his body as instantly to cure his infirmities. Christ was a means of awakening this power in that man's spirit. But Christ Himself did not give the person that power. *It was latent in the person healed.* Christ woke it into life, and probably only temporary life and activity, for we do not hear that any of the recorded cases of sudden healing in those times were permanent. They fell sick again and finally lost their bodies. Why? Because the faith or power which they drew to themselves for a brief time did not come to stay. They had not learned to increase it continually through silent demand of the Supreme Power. Their spirits went back into the domain of material belief. When that belief again materialised a load on the spirit hard to carry and they were sick, no one was at hand like the Christ to awaken it into a temporary faith or power.

No person can become permanently whole (which implies, among other powers, immortality in the flesh), or attain entire and permanent freedom from disease, who is ever trusting or leaning on any other save the Supreme to gain the power of faith. In this respect every mind must stand entirely alone. You cannot draw the highest power if you depend always for help on another or others. If you do, you are only borrowing or absorbing their faith. Such borrowed faith may work wonders for a time. But it does not come to stay. When that of which you borrow is cut off, you will fall into the slough of despond and disease again. You had really never drawn from the right source—the Supreme.

Our most profitable demand or prayer, made consciously or unconsciously, is, "Let my faith be ever increased."

When you reverse your mental attitude regarding sickness and do but entertain the belief that it is an effort of the spirit to throw off errors in thought which, as absorbed and received from earliest infancy, are materialised in your flesh, you gradually cease to load up with error. You commence also the process of unloading and casting out all former errors in thought. The sickness you had many years ago in fear of death has, in a sense, packed away that particular remembrance of such mood of fear in your being, and with it the belief that accompanied such remembrance. That belief has been working against you all these years, as all wrong belief must work against you.

It is literally a part of your real being, as all past individual remembrances and experiences are a literal part of our beings.

It is retained in your spiritual memory, although its material remembrance may have faded out. That remembrance is in thought a reality. But it is the remembrance of a false belief, teaching that death and decay can never be overcome. This belief, the reversed action and state of your mind will cast out. But such casting out must have a correspondent expression in the flesh. The physical expressions of all your former coughs and colds, fevers and other illness must reappear, at first possibly severe, but gradually in a modified form. You are then unloading your old false beliefs. But if your belief is not reversed and you go on as before, regarding physical decay and death as inevitable, then with every illness, in such mental condition, you pack away another error, another untruth and another addition to the load of untruths, whose certain effect, as added to the rest, is to weaken, crush and finally cause the body to perish.

There is no period in the " physical life " too late for receiving or entertaining the truth. There is no period too late for such truth to commence its process of physical renewal, and though that particular physical life may not be perpetuated, yet the spirit, in receiving such truth, receives a force which will be of priceless value to it on the unseen side, and by its aid it may be able the sooner to build for itself a more perfect spiritual body, and the ultimate of the relatively perfected spiritual body is the power to be and live in the physical and spiritual realms of existence at will.

If you hold to the idea that mankind are always to go on as in the past, losing their bodies, and are also to remain without the power to keep those bodies in perfect health, then you set your belief against the eternal fact that all things in this planet are ever moving forward to greater refinement, greater powers and greater possibilities.

Medicine and material remedies may greatly assist the throwing-off process. A skilled and sympathetic physician of any school may be of much assistance. Everything depends on the mind and belief in which you take the medicine and the physician's advice. If you regard both as aids to your spirit in throwing off a load and building for you a new body, you give, in such belief, great help to the spirit so to throw off and build. But if you regard both medicine and physician as aids only to the body, and a body also which you hold must at best weaken and perish some time during the next thirty, forty or fifty years, you will load up with belief in error faster than you cast it off, and the load becomes at last too heavy for the spirit to carry.

What causes the man or woman to be "bowed down by age"? What causes the stooping shoulders, the weakened knees, the tottering gait? Because we believe only in the earthly and perishable. The spirit is not earthly, nor is it perishable. But you can load it down literally with an earthly quality of thought which will "bow it down toward the earth with such burthen."

It is not the physical body of the old person that is bent and bowed down. It is that part which is the force moving the body, that is, his or her spirit, loaded with material thought which it cannot appropriate or assimilate, that becomes so bent, bowed and weak. The body is always an external correspondence of your mind or spirit.

A body thus ever renewing, beautifying, freshening and strengthening means a mind behind it ever renewing with new ideas, plans, hope, purpose and aspiration. Life eternal is not the half-dead life of extreme old age.

The person who can see only the physical side and temporary expression of life ; who eats and drinks in the belief that only the body is affected by less eating and drinking; who believes that the body is sustained merely by force generated within itself, and that it is not fed of an unseen element coming from the spiritual realm of element ; who believes that nothing exists but what he can see, hear and feel with the physical sense (that is, the material, which is always the temporary and perishable), draws to himself mostly those forces and elements which cause the temporary and perishable, and these, acting in his body, make it temporary and perishable.

Death of the body begins with thousands many years ere they are in their coffins. The pale face, with its parchment-coloured skin, means a half-dead skin. It means a portion of the body on which the spirit works the casting-out process of dead element and taking on of the new very imperfectly. In the freshness of infancy and early youth, the spirit cast out and took on more vigorously. As years went on, untruth was absorbed by that spirit. Its growth in knowledge was more and more retarded. Responding physical changes became slower and slower. The body commenced to show "signs of age," that is, to die, because such spirit was less and less fed of that element which brings constant renewal of new thought, which is new life.

So far does the belief and faith in weakness and decay prevail with the race that wisdom is often allegorically portrayed as an old man, gray, bald-headed, bowed and sustained by a staff. That means a wisdom which cannot prevent its own body from falling to pieces.

In that form of being we call the child (a spirit or mind having come into possession of a new body), there is for a period a greater spiritual wisdom than when the child is physically more matured. It is the unconscious wisdom of intuition. It is for a time more open to the truth. For such reason, up to the age of eighteen or twenty, the spiritual casting off and taking on processes in the body are more perfectly performed. These relatively rapid changes in the physical maintain the bloom and freshness of youth. Sooner or later, however, the higher spiritual process ceases gradually to operate. Beliefs in the false, as taught or absorbed from others, materialise themselves in the body, despite all the resistance of the higher mind, as expressed in pain and sickness. The load of belief in the earthy and perishable accumulates. The body assumes an appearance in correspondence with such thought. At last the higher mind refuses longer to carry such a burthen, flings it off and leaves a dead body.

The death of the body is then the final process for casting off cruder element from the spirit which it can no longer use or appropriate.

But it is very desirable for the spirit to be able

to keep a physical body which shall refine as the spirit refines, because in such equality of refinement between the spirit and its instrument, our increase in happiness is greatly advanced, and the relatively perfected rounding out of our powers cannot be realised until this union between spirit and body is effected.

When the Christ of Judea said to the elders of Israel of the little child, " Except ye become as this child ye cannot enter the Kingdom of Heaven," He meant, as the text interprets itself to us, that they should become as open to that inflowing of force as that spirit (the child) was at that period of its existence.

Were such influx maintained, the youth of the body would be perpetual.

The child is more " led of the spirit " than the grown-up person. It is more natural. It discards policy. It shows openly whom it likes and whom it does not. It has often more intuition. It will dislike a bad man or a bad woman when its parents see no evil in that person. It knows or rather feels far more regarding life than its parents give it credit for. But it cannot voice its thoughts in words. Yet the thoughts are still there. It has not learned to train itself to the double-faced custom of the world which smiles in your face and sneers behind your back. It is relatively natural. Its spirit for a time gives itself free expression. When the spirit loses this freedom of expression, when we pretend what we are not, when we say " Yes " outwardly and think " No " inwardly, when we court only to gain a favour, when we feel anger or disappointment or irritation within and pretend content and happiness without, we become **more** and more unnatural in all tastes

156

and desires.   We blunt and for a time destroy all
the higher spiritual senses and powers.   We become unable to distinguish truth from falsehood.
We are unable to feel spiritually what faith means,
much less draw this great and indispensable power
to us, and without this drawing power the physical
body must be cast off by the spirit.

The body in dying does not " give up the ghost."
It is the ghost (the spirit) that rejects the material
body.

If the spirit, through casting off unbelief, becomes more and more accessible to thoughts and
things that are true, and, therefore, grows to more
and more power, it will, acting in all parts and
functions of the body, operate the casting-off
process more and more quickly, as it does in the
material youth.   It will refuse or reject, through
the physical senses of touch or taste, anything
which would injure or adulterate it.   It can attain
to such power that an active poison, if accident-
ally placed in the mouth, would be instantly
detected and rejected, or if swallowed would be
instantly cast from the stomach.

It is not the physical stomach which rejects
food unfit for it or casts out the nauseous dose.
It is the spirit which moves the organ to such
action through a knowledge of its own that the
cast-out substance is unfit for it.   It is so unfit
because there is no spirit or quality in the rejected
element which can assimilate with and help the
spirit.   As your spirit grows in power, this sensi-
tiveness to all things which can do it evil, be they
of the seen or unseen world of things, will increase.
It grows keener and keener to the approach or
presence of everything evil and casts it off.   It
will warn you instantly of the evil or designing

person. It will tell you what is safe and fit for your association. It will at last cast out or refuse to receive all evil thoughts which now you may daily receive unconsciously, which work more harm than anything material can do, for by them the spirit is poisoned.

As faith increases many material aids will be called in by the spirit which will greatly help the renewing processes. These aids will come in selection of foods, in choosing proper associations and other changes of habit and custom.

But it is the spirit which must prompt and direct these material aids. When such prompting comes you will be obliged to follow it. The food to be avoided you will not be able to eat. Your taste will reject it. The association injurious to you, you will not be able to keep company with. The habit to be changed will drop off easily and naturally.

But if you make any rigid rules for yourself in these matters, in the hope that they will tend to spiritualise you, you are allowing the material self to take the matter in hand. The material or lower mind is then trying to give the law and rule, and to refine the spiritual or higher self. Let the spirit, increased in faith, do the work, and when the time comes for you to reject any animal food, or any of the grosser element in any form, the desire and relish for these will have gone.

In stating our belief that immortality in the flesh is a possibility, we do not infer that it is one which any now physically alive may realise. Neither do we infer that it is one which they cannot realise. Nor do we argue that people should immediately set to work in any material sense in order to " live for ever." We hold only that it is one result which must come sooner or later of that spirit evolution, or growth from the cruder to the finer, which has always been operating on this planet and on every form of matter. Matter is spirit temporarily materialised so as to be evident to correspondent physical sense.

As we grow in the faith of these spiritual processes for casting out the old and taking in the new, and consequently realise the accompanying greater refinement or spiritualisation of the body, we shall aid more and more those who are nearest us on the unseen side of life. For as we become more spiritualised in the flesh they are helped more to materialise of the spirit. In other words, we shall become physically tangible each to the other, because in the material thought which we cast off there exists an element which they can appropriate to make themselves more material. Their spiritual bodies are also under the same laws as regards the throwing off and taking on process. What they throw off as coarser to them is the finer and fit for us. This element we spiritually absorb. It is for the time and condition a certain spiritual food and life for us. Through what they throw off we are aided to spiritualise the body. Through what we throw off they are aided to materialise the spirit.

This is the end of this publication.

Any remaining blank pages are for our book binding
requirements and are blank on purpose.

To search thousands of interesting publications like this one,
please remember to visit our website at:

http://www.kessinger.net

CPSIA information can be obtained
at www.ICGtesting.com
Printed in the USA
RVHW091643070720
R3169BV00006B/646